THE REAL POWER OF
HABITS

How to Unleash Your Will Power, Break Bad Habits,
Establish Discipline, and Reach Your Goals incl.
Bonus: 30 Days Habits Transformation Planner

EDWARD C. HUGHES

TABLE OF CONTENTS

"YOU WILL NEVER CHANGE YOUR LIFE,
UNTIL YOU CHANGE SOMETHING YOU DO DAILY"
- JOHN C. MAXWELL

Habits. Bad habits are usually targeted with New Year's Resolutions in favour of good behaviours. It would be interesting to note whether these resolutions are ever successful. And if not, why not?

Every day of your life is merely a process in preparation for the next. You become as a result of whatever you do today. That means that any 30-day plan of action is only as successful as what you do today. And what you do the next day. For thirty days. What you do not need is to be overwhelmed by the plan. You develop good habits through consistent application. To make this doable, this book is designed to be read one chapter at a time, daily and then lived accordingly.

INTRODUCTION

People set themselves up for failure by believing that they are at all goal orientated. Waiting to achieve something someday is a future goal. Doing something every day is a system. Success is for the most part influenced by how well we structure such systems that effortlessly lead to progress rather than success somehow determined by in-the-moment self-control. Let me use dieting as an example that everyone can appreciate. Losing weight may be your goal. Correct eating is the system. In the sporting arena, making it to the Olympic games may be your goal, but training diligently in your chosen field is the system. Using systems is more innovative and successful because you execute the system. A goal may be your ultimate desire, but you have no control over it. Goals require ideal conditions. Systems can be put into place whenever you decide. Goals are results-oriented while systems are process-oriented. A system makes allowances for many accomplishments whereas a goal is typically an all or nothing scenario. Training at the gym 5 days a week forms part of your system to achieving your goal of becoming physically fit. Every day that you train is an achievement. You win every time you train. The best scenario for being goal-oriented is that it sets you up for pre-success failure, and permanent failure at worst.

But before we progress further, we should understand a few basics. What is a habit? What is a praxis? How about willpower? Where does that fir into the whole scheme of habits and breaking the bad ones?

What is a habit?

"Your beliefs become your thoughts,
your thoughts become your words,
Your words become your actions,
your actions become your habits,
Your habits become your values,
your values become your destiny."
– Mahatma Gandhi

Habits get us through every day. Habits should not be viewed in only a negative light, because they are mostly what makes us efficient, productive members of families, communities and societies. Almost half of the daily tasks we accomplish day in, and day out are purely habits. Can you imagine having to consciously think about your every action, every single simple thing you do every day? How much do you suppose you would actually accomplish anything? Would you even come out of it with a modicum of sanity? It is habit that gets you to work, and habits that get you through a day's work. Habits are the reason you can deal with your families and live your life every day of every week. That being said it is also true that bad habits can inhibit the realization of certain goals.

When we know what it is, we can deal with it from a place of understanding. Of course, you would ideally get to know what a habit is from different perspectives to fully understand it and then move towards breaking bad habits and developing good habits.

A habit is regular or settled tendency or practice, notably one that is hard to give up. Habits have a tendency to exits subconsciously. Let us look at a seemingly respectable daily routine that involves stopping off every weekday to buy the daily newspaper on the way to dropping the kids off at school.

Immediately you start the car, you start planning the buying of the newspaper. After so many years, it has become automatic and programmed. You make sure the correct amount of change is at hand in the car, and easily accessible to hand over to the newspaper seller at the traffic lines. You know which lane to be in to make it convenient. You say hi to the seller as you and him the change and he hands the paper through the window which you already had open in anticipation of the exchange. It has become an automatic behaviour, or a habit, if you will. Your wife has suggested you subscribe online to receive the digital version, but that just would not be the same, would it? The truth of the matter is that it would be tough for you to go digital because the buying of the newspaper at the corner has become a regular routine in your day. The reality is that you are wasting money and you do not even read most of what is in the daily paper every day. Mostly, the time you have spent over sections of the paper that do not enrich your life or interest you every day could have been spent more productively elsewhere.

Let's look at the habit of snacking. Do you have a snack in your desk drawer right now? You may have made the conscious decision to not eat unhealthy snacks. And all goes very well until that mid-morning slump hits. You missed breakfast because the alarm did not go off. Or you managed breakfast, but it was not sufficient to sustain you through the morning until lunch time. While you are hard at work getting that interim report compiled at your desk, you feel the need and before you even realize you have opened the drawer, you find that you have devoured half a packet of chocolate chip cookies. Mindless snacking, while your mind was occupied on the report. Do you see how easy it is?

From a psychology perspective, a habit is any regularly repeated behaviour that requires little or no thought and is learned rather than innate. A habit is developed through reinforcement and repetition.

Habit is in effect a three-step progression, best remembered as TRR: Trigger, Routine, and Reward.

The Trigger or Cue: the situational trigger which is grounded on the reward you're chasing.

The Reward: The satisfaction you are chasing by following the routine.

The Routine: That emotional or physical act you perform in order to earn your reward.

The trigger or cue can be a certain time of the day, a place, people, pattern of behaviour, activity, mood or emotional state of mind, or simply a thought or a belief. Your trigger or cue might be a feeling: I'm exhausted, I'm starving, I'm bored, I'm depressed. Your trigger or cue could be a time of day: it's a Monday morning, work week begins! Your cue might simply be a pattern of behaviour: go to the pub after work, sit back with a drink and a few friends and light up that smoke. If it's certain people, you could find yourself faced with the urge to smoke a joint whenever you're in the company of Joe and Mary. An activity might give you the urge to relapse into a habit, such as that weekly midweek game of tennis that always sees you overindulging at the club afterwards. Can you see how diverse the challenges could be? This external trigger, whatever it may be, has an associated habit. When you encounter the trigger, your sub-conscious behavioural pattern immediately kicks in. This basically means that your behaviour is then controlled by your subconscious mind rather than by your conscious and voluntary mindfulness. In effect the trigger pushes your buttons, so to say, which in turn leads to the acting out of a certain set of behaviour. This set of behaviour is known as routine.

And so, we come to the second step in the progression: routine, the action itself. Routine is either mental or physical. As such it is either a type of behaviour that you enact or do, or a participation in a thinking pattern that is quite rightfully also a form of action. The routine could be a negative action that you want to eliminate or decrease, such as alcohol consumption, smoking cigarettes, over-eating or spending too much time in front of the television or online or on social media. It could just as well be a positive action, such as exercising, whether it be at the gym or running outdoors, or reading books.

Whether your habit is amazing and empowering or the funnel of a negative spiral downwards, depends largely on your actions or routine. Because of the reward factor, the body is simply just after the gratification and your choice of response will inevitably become your habit just as soon as you have repeated it a sufficient number of times.

The third and final step, reward, is always as a result of routine and always follows any action. The reward can be viewed as a positive result stemming from the action or routine.

A very interesting example of the TRR three-step progression is the way in which we have been compelled by an ad man to brush our teeth. Before this ad man was approached to punt Pepsodent toothpaste, the American public already had terrible dental problems. They needed something but previous and existing types of tooth cleaners had not encouraged Joe Soap to try them out. The ad man tried many ways to market the toothpaste, to no avail. The ad man, Hopkins, eventually tried altruistic advertising. He had happened upon the right human psychology, and it was so simple, it had two basic rules:

1. Find a cue

   In the Pepsodent example the cue was the film everyone finds on their teeth, especially first thing in the morning. This plaque build-up has always been around, but no one had brought it to the attention of the public until the ad man found a way to use it to sell Pepsodent. Just run your tongue across your teeth. Do you feel it? This is exactly the motivator used by the ad man for the public to find the cue.

2. define the reward

   A sparkling smile and beautiful teeth. Contemporary toothpastes contain refreshing substances such as peppermint which actually do nothing to aid the cleaning process. They add a secondary reward: a tingling sensation that convinces you that you have a minty fresh mouth.

By simply using a cue that was and always had been around, the ad man found his trigger, and it sparked toothpaste to be used ritually every morning and every day, for the promise of a clean beam.

Habit formation is the result of the mechanics of trigger, routine, and reward. You are increasingly compelled by the reward to automatically repeat the routine whenever the trigger occurs. Subconsciously you are ever more sure that you will be rewarded by the habit, and so you repeat the behaviour. Once formed, the habit forms its own neural network in the brain which is strengthened by repetition and which weakens if not acted on. Much like a muscle that is encouraged by exercising, and atrophies when it is no longer flexed and used, but which never actually disappears. The code in the brain will always be there, however, even long after the activity is discontinued. The routine will continue to be whenever the external trigger is encountered.

If the brain is so to say hot-wired to behave in response to a trigger, are we not pretty much at the mercy of the habit for the rest of our lives? When one considers genius marketing campaigns, behavioural psychology, bad genes, and an environment that consistently sets up for failure, are we not also quite thoroughly ruled by bad habits?

No. By forming a new habit and making sure it is strong enough that you can use it to disregard the old habit, you can change your habits.

What is a praxis?

While a 30-day plan to break a habit, unleash willpower, and set goals requires practicing the theory, it is nonetheless important to know to a certain extent the theory behind the practice in order to achieve the goal.

Praxis is defined by the Oxford Dictionary as a noun:

practice, as distinguished from theory.
«modern political praxis is now thoroughly permeated
with a productivist ethos»
accepted practice or custom.
«patterns of Christian praxis in Church and society»

Which doesn't really explain why this 30-day plan is a praxis and not merely theoretical. The Cambridge Dictionary is slightly more helpful in defining praxis according to our requirements:

the process of using a theory or something that you have
learned in a practical way:
She is interested in both the theory and praxis of criminology

The 30 day plan can be viewed as a form of Personal Development Project (PDP) with regularly scheduled tasks to be completed within 30 days in a way that the objectives, tasks, and achievements can be revisited beyond the 30 days, for as long as you need to in order to break every selected habit, one at a time, over a reasonable period. The objective is to accomplish clear, traceable outcomes on your journey to become a better version of yourself. The purpose in a nutshell is to assist you to achieve four basic goals:

- committing to challenging tasks to achieve resultant skill development (break bad habit and replace it with healthy habit)

- to achieve self-confidence and a sense of accomplishment through consistently completing set goals

- self-actualization resultant from repetitive positive action

- eventual predisposition to behave according to the rules originally set to achieve the initial goal

A praxis in the form of a 30-day planner will make it easier to make an idea or concept real and to give specific or definite form to your goal through prioritized steps so that you attain what you actually want.

By making each step easy to achieve, the barriers are broken down so that you essentially take baby steps daily, then weekly, until you reach your target. While long term goals are kind of pie-in-the-sky, targets over 30 days set out in small steps are easier to stick to, leading to a sense of accomplishment every 30 days. Daily and weekly action leaves us little wiggle room but to start now. 30 days seems perfect since it is neither too short in which to produce real results or too long, which opens you up to falling into the New Year's Resolutions trap.

How to use the 30-day planner:

- Once you have decided on the habit you want to break (goal), dissect the goal into an activity that can be completed daily. Using the goal of writing a 60-thousand-word book as example, commit to writing 2000 words every single day for 30 days. Now, doesn't that look way more achievable than merely setting yourself up to the intimidating task of having to somehow write 60-thousand words in a month?

- Concentrate on the process rather than just your eventual result. After you have reached your 30-day target, commit to other daily tasks that will either help to set your original goal in stone, or to break another habit.

This book endeavours to explain the theory behind habits and attaining goals using willpower, among other useful psychological and practical means, to be able to practically implement the 30-day plan better. The surmise that 'if you know better, you will do better' comes into play.

Willpower explained

Willpower can be described as similar to a muscle which can be worn out with overuse. It will be increasingly difficult to resist temptations with a tired-out willpower. Days of constant and unrelenting stress and skirmishes with your own thoughts and feelings will have you capitulating before every temptation that stands in your way.

Your will is your ability to make conscious choices, and it is through free will that you get to decide for yourself, which may simply mean that you choose to do as you are told. Free will. Apparently, we are the only one of earth's creations that have full command of will. We only outdo animals and plants in this regard because we excel at thinking and making informed decisions. It is all well and good knowing that you can achieve 'at will', but then those pesky obstacles get put in your path and suddenly all the more will is required to act as you choose. Will is directly correlated with desire. You can attest to this if you have ever tried out for something you really wanted as compared to half-heartedly tried at something. With desire comes persistence and the cliché 'Where there's a will, there's a way' starts to make a great deal more sense.

The application of will as self-control is really just the conflict of desire. What then is self-control? Self-control is the ability to moderate behaviour, impulse, and emotion in order to realize long-term goals. The prefrontal cortex of the human brain is where self-control is managed. This decision-making, problem-solving and planning centre of the brain is responsible for willpower, in effect because it is through this rich concoction of nerve connections that people get to avoid getting into situations they may live to regret and are able to delay immediately responding to every impulse. It is this self-control that puts contemporary humans on a different plain to animals. This ability to exercise self-control is what we call will-power. Willpower to act and react in a certain way despite stimuli. Our motivation to practice will is what we know as willpower. Strong willpower allows for a decision despite many obstacles to achievement. Weak willpower will present in the person who gives up easily in the face of opposition. The correlation between will and power is strong. See the exercising of will as a show of power. Powerful people are usually seen as having a strong will.

Self-control is a major factor to breaking a habit because it is important to have self-belief or confidence in your own willpower when you are attempting to break a bad habit. Belief in yourself makes it way easier to break a bad habit.

Where does willpower come into breaking habits? When you are forced to exercise, it will be easy for you to abandon the effort just as soon as you have a viable excuse, you are too busy, or it is raining. Same applies to motivation. If you must be motivated to succeed, it is easy to give up. This is because willpower and motivation are finite and both fickle, and they will forsake you when needed most. Motivation and willpower alone are not enough to break bad habits and replace them with healthy habits.

THE PSYCHOLOGY BEHIND BAD HABITS

We are what we repeatedly do. Excellence,
then, is not an act, but a habit

– Aristotle

When you have bad habits to get rid of, you very quickly appreciate the impact the brain has on whether or not you will be successful. That is the brain as well as the cognitive connection. For this reason, behavioural psychology is a great help and can give you the all-important and necessary perception of how to break bad habits and replace them with healthy habits. The chief reason for behaviour to be repeated until it becomes a habit comes down to the reward aspect. As touched on before, the reward is the final phase in the three-step progression mentioned as TRR: Trigger – Response – Reward. Bad habits are always adopted because of the reward you receive after performing the act.

We can illustrate this using the emotional eater as an example. The habitual eater reacts to stress with food. The food is the reward that instantly gratifies the eater in a stressful situation.

Since we are dealing with the psychological phenomenon that is conditioning, we simply must introduce you to Pavlov and his dogs at this stage. Ivan Pavlov was a Russian scientist back in the last few years of the 19th century. His interest was in the workings of the digestive system in mammals, but his experiment inadvertently led to a better understanding of the psychological school of thought involving what was termed classical conditioning. Pavlov had assistants working with the dogs in his experiment who were responsible also for presenting the dogs with their food. These assistants all wore lab coats. The studies involved identifying what triggered the dogs to salivate because mammals use saliva as a step in digesting food. But the study presented surprising results in that the dogs did not only salivate when presented with their food. They also very soon into the study showed the tendency to salivate whenever they saw a person wearing a lab coat, even though there was no food in sight. To get an answer to this reaction, Pavlov rang a bell whenever the dogs were fed. Pretty soon, the dogs were drooling at the sound of the bell, also in the absence of any food. The summation was that the dogs were demonstrating classical conditioning. This is why:

- The bell was a neutral stimulus because it did not cause any reaction or response on its own.

- The food was the non-neutral, or unconditioned stimulus, which produced salivation.

- Salivation was the unconditioned response.

- The dogs salivating at the sound of the bell is the conditioned response.

By presenting the dogs with both the neutral stimulus and the unconditioned stimulus simultaneously, the dogs will over time associate the two. Due to this association, the dogs will respond to the neutral stimulus in the same way as they do to the unconditioned stimulus, even when it is presented on its own. This is known as a conditioned response.

So now we know that dogs can be conditioned or trained to behave in a certain way. What about people? John Watson was a psychologist who founded the behaviourism school of thought back in the early 1900s. He experimented on a 9-month old baby boy by the name of Albert to prove his belief that human behaviour occurs primarily in the context of conditioning. Albert was not afraid of rats at the outset of what was to be titled the Little Albert Experiment. He exhibited only a curious response when presented with the rat. This response was replaced by one of fear only after some time, after Watson made a loud noise behind the baby boy on different occasions while simultaneously showing him the rat. It did not take long for Albert to cry when he saw the rat even without the loud noise. Albert had been content with the presence of the rat, he had however cried when experiencing the loud noises. By associating the rat with the scary loud noise, Albert became conditioned to cry when presented with the rat alone, in the absence of any noise. In effect, Albert was trained to cry at the presence of a rat.

According to behavioural psychologists, whatever we do behaviour-wise is either punished or rewarded. Depending on whether the behaviour is rewarded or punished, the likelihood of the behaviour ever being repeated either decreases or increases. The answer to breaking the bad habit therefore becomes identifying the way in which you are rewarded by your bad habit, and then finding a workable way to replace that habit.

Again, easier said than done, you say. But it really is as easy as being mindful of your act actions and behaviour and having the willpower to break the habits you no longer want in your life. You will have to want to break the cycle of rewarding your bad habit, which takes commitment. Commitment is rewarded or penalized, depending on whether you react best to positive or negative reinforcement. I deal with this in more depth in the 30-day plan. Suffice to say that you can either choose to relinquish a reward when you relapse or castigate yourself using a negative stimulus appropriate to the behaviour. The payoff according to behavioural psychology, for any behaviour, is the reward. For this reason, it makes sense that you should reward yourself frequently when you are trying to break a bad habit. You cannot be restrictive or irregular in your doling out of appropriate rewards. Every good act must be rewarded.

The reward must match the behaviour, though. A big reward for a major achievement and a respectively token reward for smaller acts of obeyance. By way of example, let us say that your lifestyle has become too sedentary and you need to tone your body back into shape. You have figured out that you immediately hit the couch when you get home from the office. You have identified the time and the location that trigger your bad habit, which will help a great deal in overcoming the bad habit. Instead of heading straight home from work, stop off at the gym and walk on the treadmill for 10 to 30 minutes. You can build this up over time. Or drive to the beach or a park, where it is safe and easy to take an invigorating walk. If the fresh air is not reward enough, buy yourself a fun water bottle featuring an amusing anecdote or a motivational phrase, as a reward that you can take along on your future walks.

A problem shared is a problem halves, so the cliché goes. Sharing your goals as far as pursuing the task of breaking your bad habit can be a form of reward and penalization in itself. When you make the decision to break a habit, tell someone important to you, or someone who may be an enabler of some kind. Whoever you decide to bring into your circle in this endeavour, please make sure that they will be fully supportive. What you do not need is a soul who might encourage you to engage in your old habit or ridicule you for failing in any way. When it is known that you are on the path to self-improvement in this way, the shame of failure becomes an effective penalty.

Which brings us to having a replacement habit waiting in the wings for its cue. Always and without fail. The replacement habit must bring you the same kind of reward that the bad habit offers, or it is just not going to be effective. If you spend too much time scrolling through social media, find out what reward that brings you. It might be that you learn something from the posts. That being the case, try reading a book of facts when you have the urge to turn to social media. If you need to change the location for this, it would be a great help to hang a hammock outside or on your deck, in which to laze while you are reading. Or you might opt rather to watch a documentary on television or online.

THE 30-DAY PLAN

*"Habit is habit, and not to be flung out of the window
by any man, but coaxed downstairs a step at a time."*

– Mark Twain

This plan is fairly simple. Simple does not however translate to easy. Although some habits are easier to break, and in the same vein, easier to set, others are relatively harder.

Choose one habit you want to break. Only one! Breaking old habits and developing healthy habits is not at all easy. We are all Pavlov's dogs, whether we like it or not. This is because every time we do something (e.g. scroll through social media when we are bored) the neuronal circuit supporting that habit becomes stronger. The habit is not just difficult to overcome, it is maintained by circuits of neurons firing in your brain. These habits in turn strengthen the neuronal circuits. A self-fulfilling behavioural loop that works both ways. The Hebbian theory states: "Neurons that fire together wire together."

Instant gratification is not the way in which the human brain is wired, though. Just like it took time to create the network of neurons in your brain to establish the habit, so too does it take time to create a habit to replace that habit. What you need is to work at it every day for 30 days, until your brain is rewired.

Some challenging habits may need more than 30 days to change and replace with healthier alternatives. If you know that at the outset, you will not be disappointed when you have not completely kicked the bad habit after 30 days. This is why it is important to set a start date ahead of time rather than jumping in both guns firing on the very same day as you decide to break your bad habit. Go for 60 days, if you think that will do the trick. Do you suppose that 90 days is too long to achieve something that will liberate you for the rest of your life, if done right? No, definitely not. Take all the time you need, provided you are committed and goal oriented and motivated to complete the tasks and take each step that is required to achieve the desired and planned for end result.

It is quite imperative that you have a strategy going in and that you maintain a workable strategy to keep yourself on track, even after the 30 days have come and gone. So, let's look at a strategy that you can work with:

Strategy # 1: Concentrate on Just One Bad Habit at a Time

It is a psychological fact that willpower has a certain limited energy in each day. This also has a psychological term attached to it, and that is 'ego depletion'. Exceeding your willpower supply makes impulse control all the more difficult. This affects habit changing and development when you try to tackle more than one habit at the same time since every habit requires as much of your willpower as you have to spend. Without the necessary willpower energy to spend on so many habits that you want to break, you fall into what is called a depleted state. Once depleted, you are running on empty, and so you simply abandon all attempts at standing up to your bad habits. The what-the-hell mindset wins out. I'll explain this mindset to you in the chapter introducing the 30-day plan and strategize on it at the end of the plan. If you just had one habit to break at a time, you would have more than enough willpower energy to tackle it and win the battle.

Let us use the battle against fizzy drinks as our illustration here. Go simple and keep it small. You are currently consuming 2 litres of coke a day. Your goal is to cut back to no coke within 30 days. Great. During week 1 work on minimizing your cola to 1.5 litres. During the second week, drop to 1 litre, and then down to 500ml in the third week. By week 4 you will be good to go with just a small glass of cola, and then you will be ready to go without it entirely by day 30. Small steps. Great results.

Strategy # 2: Identify your target goal

If you did not know it before, you know it now. Breaking a bad habit is exactly the same as setting a goal. Without a definite outcome in mind and a certain target date, you are not going to successfully break any bad habits. Be specific in identifying your goal. You don't want to just say that you want to lose weight. This is not a specific target at all. Identify why it is that you have a problem with your weight. Make a note of the foods that you know are responsible for your weight problem. Write them down. Write down a very specific goal: As of 14 February, I will be cooking only healthy, nutritious meals, with a combination of fresh vegetables, protein and healthy carbs. I will not be eating fast food or junk food at all, and no more fizzy drinks.

Strategy # 3: No Going Cold Turkey

It is just not often possible for a mere mortal to decide never to engage in a bad habit ever again as of right now, and then success-fully do just that. It does happen, this is true. People have kicked a habit cold turkey and gone on to never relapse. But the fail-ures are too many and the success stories are really minimal. The biggest obstacle to quitting cold turkey, is the lack of wiggle-room.

Focusing on perfection is a dangerous way to quit a bad habit. The pursuit of perfection usually just results in developing a "what the hell" mindset. This mindset follows closely on the heels of breaking the never-again-rule that is synonymous with going cold turkey. Subconsciously a decision is inevitably made that since they have already slipped up, a good old binge is in order. What comes as a result of the "what the hell" is more engaging in the bad habit than would ordinarily have been the case. The possibility of slip ups is just too great, and you have to give yourself room to fail, to pick up the pieces, get back on the wagon, and try again. Temptation is in the bible. That is how long people have been subject to it and its nasty little way of pulling the carpet out from under the unsuspecting and the vulnerable. This is more often than not, certainly a proven technique on how best not to change a routine.

The strategy continues throughout the 30-day plan, so keep an eye out for a continuation hereof throughout the book.

Day Zero:
Pre-plan Preparation

Most important before you embark on your 30-day plan, is to bear in mind to keep it simple. Also make it a small habit. This is very definitely not the time to go big or go home. Changing your habit should never be complicated. Consistency is key! Consistency is of way more importance than intensity. When you prove to yourself over a month or more that you have successfully engaged in your replacement habit, this is the point at which you up the intensity. Do not go ninja during the first 30 days, you will have plenty of 30 days to come after your first and initial successful 30-day plan is done and dusted.

You need to get your new habit realized in a way that you are indubitably confident of sticking with it over the duration and then forever after. It is absolutely ideal that you make your new replacement habit one that is significant for you. You will have to commit to this new habit. First for the foreseeable few months, and then years, and eventually all your life. You will want to start small, and then you can endure. When you know that you can do a little, then you can do that every day.

If you are one of those people who do not know how to go small, I have some examples of tiny habits to give you an idea.

- To instil that eating plan that will stay with you for the rest of your life, just start with eating a nutritious breakfast. And then do it again on day 2.

- To implement your fitness plan that will be a part of your life forever more, start with one sit up.

Write down what your tiny habit will be. All you need to know to break a habit and ingrain new behaviour is given in tip-form here.

The simple steps to successfully ingrain a habit and change a habit:

1. Step 1: Put your plan down on paper. Write it all down because you will have to refer to the plan throughout the 30 days and for a long time beyond.

2. Step 2: Identify your triggers and your replacement habits.

3. Step 3: Mindfully concentrate on implementing your replacement habits over the 30 days, whenever you encounter your triggers, for about 30 days.

As mentioned, strategies help to achieve goals. Strategies to breaking habits will be provided throughout the book.

Strategy # 4: Set Your Start Date

Decide on a doable start date and then write it down. It will help to broadcast your goal and your intention to your support system. We elaborate further on your support system and how to deal with them later in the plan. A good reason behind having a start date is the energy it provides. You should be excited and motivated by having committed to a start date.

Strategy # 5: Focus on Daily Increases in Improvement

Wean yourself off of your bad habit by concentrating on increment improvements every single day for 30 days. This is how you can be certain you will successfully make that permanent change. Set your target goals and then steadily reduce your engagement in the bad habit, until you have eliminated it completely. We have already ascertained how quitting cold turkey isn't realistic for long-term success, so you have the knowledge to set your sights on incremental goals. What you are going to do is slowly move away from engaging in your bad habit. This means that if you want to lose weight you will have to set a goal weight and then work on bringing down the number on your bathroom scale every day, consistently and diligently over the 30 days. If you want to get fit and no longer lead an unhealth sedentary lifestyle, commit to a definite time of mindless leisure, whether it is watching television, surfing the net, or scrolling social media. Now cut down on the time spent doing these mindless sedentary activities, until you reach the allocated time. Do you want to quit drinking fizzy cooldrinks? Set a target of nil cooldrinks by day 25, (or whatever works for you) and then reduce your intake of sodas every day until you reach the target.

Cheat sheet for breaking a habit:

1. Only tackle one habit at a time. You really need to concentrate on one at a time if you want to be successful or else you will almost certain fail.

2. Start off small and grow with time. Breaking a habit is not easy, so you need to take it slowly. Don't go cold turkey with giving up an 'addiction' and don't jump in the deep end with both feet. If you want to get fit, don't sign up for a triathlon until you are fit enough. If you want to give up drinking, wean yourself off alcohol over time, with the right support system already in place to get you through.

3. Don't start immediately. You will want a start date and a quit date. Specifically noting these on a wall- or desk-planner gives it more significance and builds the anticipation and excitement. Once you have these dates, broadcast it to everyone you feel needs to know. You will definitely need a note pad to write down your plan and anything else that will help you to break the habit you have decided needs to be changed.

4. Always make a note of the habit you want to break–write it down on paper. Speaking it is not a true and real commitment.

5. Write down your plan to make sure that you are sufficiently prepared. Include the motivation behind your habit change, possible obstacles, triggers, support system and friends, and your means to succeed. More on this later. Just write it down!

6. This plan is over 30 days because it takes about that long to break a habit and replace it with a better one. But you have to concentrate on it and remain consistent. Of course, every person is different, and you may need more time to get it right. Habits are also variable, and some habits may be easier and less time consuming to change than others. There is no right or wrong number of days in which to break a habit.

7. Write down your motivation in your plan and make certain it is strong. Your reasons for wanting to break this habit must be crystal clear in your own mind. Same goes for the benefits of being successful in breaking the habit.

8. Be prepared for minefields. Make a written note of the obstacles you will face when trying to change your habit. This includes obstacles you have already encountered and obstacles you are likely to run into this time around. Reflect on your past failures, in the event you have tried to break this habit before. Reflection will help you to ascertain why

you failed. Now make a note of your strategies to overcome the obstacles.

9. Identify all the situations that trigger your bad habit. Some habits have more than one trigger. Write them all down in your plan.

10. Write down your replacement habits. Once you have identified and written down your triggers, add a positive habit you plan to replace it with. Positive habits are exercise, meditation, deep breathing, and mindful pauses.

11. Into you plan, write down the names of the people (I like to call them habit-heroes) who will form your support system. You need the right person or people to be in your corner when you are faced with a strong urge. You can find support forums online which are very helpful as a tool to break certain habits.

12. Be accountable. This must be a public accountability. Post your success and failures on a forum or tell your support buddy.

13. Continuously renew your commitment. Read your plan as many times as you need to. Recommit every day, in the morning and at night, and as many times in between as you need to.

14. Over and above your support system you need to know that you have the support of your family, friends and co-workers. You have to be able to ask for help. Your supporters need to know how important it is to you that you have their full support. AA groups and online forums are worth their weight in gold when you are finding the going hard. Sign up and use whatever support networks and systems you have access to.

15. Self-talk is vitally important. It is omnipresent and omnipotent. Know this and use it to help you instead of letting it be an obstacle. Self-talk occurs almost all the time, but you are very likely to be totally oblivious to it. Start to pay attention if you have any hope of breaking that habit. Be your own cheerleader. Repeat your mantra to yourself and listen to those pep talks you give yourself. Unfortunately, your inner dialogue is typically negative rather than helpful. Thoughts in the tone of "I can't do this" or "I'm not strong enough" are more than enough to dash all your hopes of success. Negative thoughts are dangerous. You simply must kill them and replace them with a positive thought. "I can do this" and "I am strong enough to beat this".

16. Strategize when urges assault you. Use your support networks and support forums. Always take it one urge at a time.

17. Visualization is really powerful for changing habits successfully. Visualization is no more than picturing yourself mentally in your own head changing your habit. Seeing yourself practicing your replacement habit whenever you experience your triggers and overcoming those urges will give you a clear view of a successful new you.

18. Reward yourself regularly. You need this positive feedback so add them to your plan.

19. Be consistent. When breaking the bond between a habit and a trigger and creating a new bind to form that replacement habit, don't make allowances. For these 30 days, do not allow yourself to make any exceptions. You need to replace every trigger whenever they come along.

20. Make it hard for you to fail. Get on track in a way that makes it difficult to fall off the wagon. Up the positive feedback when you follow the plan. Up the negative feedback when you do not. Failures are very likely. Don't despair. It is easier to push through when you plan for things to go wrong. Figure out what the problem was and deal with it in case it happens again. Overcome every obstacle because you are worth it.

Days One, Two and Three: Mental Preparedness

Do you have the commitment required to break your habit?

Yes.

Great.

Ask yourself what your primary motivation is for breaking this bad habit. If you can make the decision to break your habit not because of guilt or shame or from a perspective of failure, but from a place of personal strength and confidence, then you are on the right track from the get-go. What you need to do is see to it that the habit becomes part of a greater cause that is worth the effort. Rather than making your replacement habit going to the gym, see it as toning your body so that you can wear your favourite dress or jeans – the ones that made you feel like the world was your oyster when you wore it or them. Instead of seeing it as getting out of bed earlier every morning, see it as making the time to get those extra jobs submitted so that you can save the money for that family holiday.

Intrinsic motivation is your strongest form of commitment. That motivation from within, whether you see it as your drive, decisiveness, or quite simply your very own fierce power, must be as a result of a reason or a desire. The personal conviction that causes you to pick a path at a crossroads when all you have is your inner compass and that is all that matters. Motivation is born through the realization that pursuing a certain habit has resultant negative effects, and clearly seeing that there are advantages to breaking that habit. To have this power, all you need is to understand what drives your bad habit. Does the habit somehow fill a need or bridge a gap or solve some or other problem? Does it make you feel better to behave in accordance with the habit? Do you feel more important, in control or likeable, perhaps even lovable, by doing it? Do you feel less bored, less alone, less abandoned, less lost?

Or does it make you feel bad about yourself? Guilty, shameful, ashamed, undeserving, self-contemptuous?

When you delve into this question, you will know that the answer that causes you the most pain and discomfort, is the one that holds most water. You must come to that place where your habit is no longer a comfort zone but an unbearable position in which to remain.

The best motivation will always make you feel in control, authentic, and positive about your decision. You must be able to stand strong in your decision despite the odds being stacked against you. You must accept that you will come up against the odds fairly often and with regular efficacy while you are trying to push forward with breaking your habit. Chocolate donuts when you're motivated to drop weight and inches by your wedding, a pub full of smokers when you have quit smoking, or an invitation to the local casino when you are fighting a gambling addiction. Just remember that with the right motivation and the commitment, you cannot be weakened, and habits will no longer have the power over you. Because you are the master of your fate.

You do not want to pit yourself up against replacing a habit with one that you loathe.

Always select a replacement habit that you can get behind. If you do not like going to gym, then do not decide on cutting back on sedentary time by spending time slogging it out in the gym. You are more likely to fail if you know at the outset that you do not like the goal that you are striving to achieve. It can however be done if you look at the end product rather than the process. You might even get to liking the gym if you can see your body improving as a result of the work you are putting into perfecting and toning it. You have the option though of rather indulging in a pastime you enjoy in order to meet your goal. Take up cross country hiking or walking along the beach with your dogs, or you could even sign up for martial arts lessons or weekly dance classes.

Another way of getting into a dislike activity is by using the technique known as temptation bundling. No, I am not just making his up. The term as well as the concept were coined by Katherine Milkman, behavioural economist and an assistant professor at Wharton University of Penn. She advocates temptation bundling as a means of effectively killing two birds with one stone. It very cleverly involves doing what you should be doing together with what you want to do. In this way you use rewards to kickstart your will-power to do what you should be doing. In this way you are getting your guilty pleasures and instant gratification while achieving the good things that are nonetheless less fun for you to do. A great example is watching downloads of your Netflix favourites while you are exercising on the orbital elliptical trainer or stationary bike.

Step 1: Awareness

You cannot plan awareness; you have to come to it as a matter of course. But it forms the basis of what will become your plan. The first step to change is being aware that change is required. Acknowledging that you have a bad habit or that you want to change a habit, is vitally important in the great scheme of the 30-day plan. In fact, without it, you would not have need of a plan whatsoever. So, well done if you have identified a habit that you want to break or change.

Some people have to hit rock bottom before they are ready to admit to having a dangerous or debilitating habit. These motivators to quit the habit may be physical. It could come in the form of the diagnosis of cancer for a chain smoker, or onset of cirrhosis in an alcoholic. The motivator could stem from a relationship, in the form of the dissolution of a family or a divorce as a result of cruelty brought on by habitual drug-abuse. Emotional motivators include posting on social media to get the 'high' of positive responses in the form of likes and comments. When you learn that these 'rewards' are only superficial, you can break the habit of checking your mobile phone throughout the day. You can also be motivated financially. Sex addicts squandering their income on paid escorts will soon deplete the financial resources to fuel the habit and have to face up to their situation.

Write it down

BY making a note of how you fall victim to your bad habit, you are not so much attempting to push down the impulse as much as merely raising awareness. If you are aware, the reward-seeking part of the brain is subdued to the extent that you do not have to react automatically, like Pavlov's dogs. You are given the ability and the mindfulness to make more conscious choices.

So write this down:

1. Write down the top ten negative side effects of your bad habit

2. Write down the top ten positive changes that would come with breaking this bad habit

3. Write down the top ten excuses you would typically fall back on to justify your bad habit

Now read it every day if you need to. It is imperative that you persevere until you have ten items in each list. By listing these ten notes in each respect, an impression will be made in your own mind explaining the reasons you simply must break your bad habit.

You have not finished with the making of notes. During this first half of your first week, you will not attempt to break your habit. Before you can work at breaking the habit, you absolutely must develop your self-awareness about what your triggers are, both the internal and the external triggers. To this end, you must task yourself to take note of and be aware where and when you fall victim to your bad habit:

- At what time/s of the day/night?

- Where are you?

- Who are you with? Are you with someone?

- What triggers the start of the behaviour?

- How do you feel immediately prior to falling prey to the habit?

- How do you feel physically both during and after giving in to the bad habit?

So now you have highlighted the cue to your habit.

Strategy # 6: Write in an Accountability Journal

Keep track of all you are doing to break your bad habit and replace it with a healthy habit. Include all the information necessary, because this will make it better for you to appreciate the impulses that affect you as well as the variance in your moods along the way. Your accountability journal should include details such as:

- How many times you engage in your bad habit

- How much time you give to engaging in your bad habit

- What are you feeling? Detail your emotions, feelings and the impulses that affect you

- What obstacles and challenges have you come up against?

To illustrate let us use the habit of too much involvement on social media. Your journal should have notes of your target or goal of the maximum time you want to spend on social media by the end of your 30-day plan. Make a note every day of the time you spent on social media during that day. Also make a detailed note of how you felt and the impulses and urges that caused you to engage on social media on that day.

Strategy # 7: You Need Your Very Own Accountability Partner

Change can be hard. It is a road best travelled in good company. If you know of anyone who wants to make the same kind of changes that you are embarking on, that is great. Someone who will appreciate your aspirations, where you are at and where you want to be. But most of all a person who can understand the road you will have to travel to get to where you are wanting to be. You need to be in frequent contact with this person while you are on your journey of lasting change. Make a commitment to meet as often as you feel is necessary, or better still tackle the mission as a team. Do it together every day if necessary. If you want to lose weight, you could go to gym together or commit to walking a certain distance together every day or every other day for the 30 days. If you do not have such a person, a sponsor would also do. As long as you have an account-ability partner, it does not even matter if they are only in your life on social media. If you can help each other, you should do so.

Strategy # 8: Go Public

Social approval is a powerful tool to changing behaviour. It is human nature not to want to appear to be a failure. Use social networks to get the support you need from your friends while you are trying to break your bad habit and replace it with a healthy habit. You can post daily or even weekly updates of your progress and your failures to garner inspiration from your followers. Linking your fitness apps and digital food diary to your social media will help you remain accountable, too.

Task 1

1. Have a journal designated to breaking the habit and write down everything during the 30 days.

2. Write down the habit you have selected to break.

3. Submit your detailed plan to paper because you will have to refer to the plan throughout the 30 days and for a long time beyond. Include:

   a. possible obstacles,

   b. triggers,

   c. support system

   d. support buddies, and

   e. how you plan to succeed

4. What is your primary motivation for breaking this bad habit? Write it down.

5. Write down the top ten negative side effects of your bad habit

6. Write down the top ten positive changes that would come with breaking this bad habit

7. Write down the top ten excuses you would typically fall back on to justify your bad habit

8. Develop your self-awareness about what your internal and the external triggers are. Take note of and be aware of where and when your bad habit is triggered:

   a. At what time/s of the day/night?

b. Where are you?

c. Who are you with? Are you with someone?

d. What triggers the start of the behaviour?

e. How do you feel immediately before the urge to engage in the habit?

f. F. How do you feel physically both during and after giving in to the urge?

9. Make a separate list of the possible obstacles you mentioned in (3) above. Beside each, note what you will do to minimize or avoid them.

10. Read your list and your plan as often as you need to until you have an impression in your own mind explaining your reasons for having to break your bad habit.

Days Four and Five:
Setting Yourself Up or Dress for Success

You literally can change your appearance to help you succeed in breaking a habit. If you look the part, you will be more confident. The more confident you are, the more likely you are to succeed.

1. Get plenty of rest so that your energy is not depleted when you really need it to resist the urge to go for the reward rather than secure the new habit.

2. Drink plenty of fresh water. Staying hydrated is important. Dehydration allows the brain to more easily give in to failure.

3. Concentrate on perfecting your posture because there is a strong link between the brain and bad posture. You can improve the brain's function by correcting your posture, which in turn improves your mood. Power poses made up of a confident stance and upright posture positively affects decision-making while subconsciously convincing your brain that you are confident, powerful, in charge, and in control of your choices.

Task 2:

1. Decide the optimal amount of sleep you need nightly to perform at your peak. Write it down in your designated journal. Tip – it should be no less than 7 hours and no more

than 9 hours. Write down the amount of sleep you get every night

2. How much water do you usually drink? If it is less than 500ml, make a commitment to increase it to at least 1250ml before moving onto the next phase, and up to 2000ml within the week. Make a note of the amount of water you drink every day.

3. Write down the steps you will take to improve your posture and check against it every day.

Days Six, Seven and Eight: Address Those Triggers

Review the notes that you made during the Awareness Stage in days one through three and pay attention to your main triggers because recognizing them is vitally essential if you are going to do the work over the rest of the 30 days. These main triggers are place, emotion, people, and times of the day.

Once you understand your habit loop and the actions that get you from trigger or cue to reward, you can get started on permanently changing your lifestyle. You will want to do this slowly and systematically if you want to make a lasting change. Imprint your bad habits with your replacement or healthy habit, or a new routine. In this way you will still get the reward but without the negative behaviour. Different routines that lead to the same rewards. Win/win.

Every habit is the same in the way it progresses. Every habit follows exactly the same three-step process:

The Cue or situational trigger that is grounded on your desired reward;

The Reward which is your pay off for going with the routine;

The Routine is whatever emotional or physical action or behaviour you engage in in order to reach the reward.

Step 2: Find the Trigger

Life is defined by what we think and do repeatedly, not by what we think and do only every now and again. So it follows that developing the right type of habit and breaking bad habits should precede any transformative effort. It is imperative you find out what triggers your undesirable habit. Some habits have more than one trigger. Once you have identified your triggers, make a note of them. Write them all down. Smokers often find social situations to be a trigger. Whether it is having drinks in a pub, joining the girls for a girls-night-out, driving your car, or that first cup of coffee when you wake in the morning.

Step 3: Identify the Habit Routine

Your habit routine is whatever behaviour satisfies whatever the trigger is that causes your urge to reach the reward. By following the routine, you either earn the reward or some form of gratification or the elimination of whatever stress is caused by that cue.

Strategy # 9: Write Down Your Bad Habit Triggers

To address your bad habits, you must know what triggers the urge to engage in the behaviour that has become the habit. It could be a sound or a smell or seeing something specific. It could also be something within yourself, a feeling or an emotion or a memory that somehow gives rise to the urge. To understand your triggers and why they happen, you need to identify and keep a note of the following when you come up against the urge to engage in a bad habit:

- Location: Write down where you are

- Time: Write down the exact time of the urge

- Mood: Make a note of the specifics of how you are feeling and your emotion

- People: Make a note of the people/person who is with or around you

- Action: Write down whatever it is you were doing in that moment or whatever you are currently engaged in

For this exercise to be of any value to you in your quest to break your bad habit, you must repeat it and concentrate on writing down all five points every time you are triggered. After a while you will see a pattern emerging as far as your bad habit is concerned. To illustrate this, let us use the situation of quitting smoking. After journaling your triggers and systematically keeping record of the above, you may find:

- Location: At work behind your desk

- Time: Noon

- Mood: Tense

- People: The receptionist is at her post in the reception area which is alongside your office

- Action: Paperwork and computer work at your desk

You will soon see a pattern emerge, that whenever the reception-ist indicates to you her intention to visit the smoking area outside your office building, you are overwhelmed with the urge, usually when stressing about the job at hand, to have a cigarette.

You soon note that your trigger is spurred during a time of stress by your desire to join the receptionist when she has a smoke.

Strategy # 10: Change up Your Rewards

The subconscious reward in the above example is a temporary reprieve from a tense situation through joining a friend for a ciga-rette. If you can determine what would be an appropriate substitute for the bad habit, you can still get your reward only through a pos-itive result.

Visualize various strategies to try out every time you come upon a trigger until you find a positive routine that leads to the same feeling your bad habit rewards you with, only without the negative routine.

Using the same illustration as above, you now know that smoking with your friend offers you a reprieve from a tense work environ-ment while also offering a chance to relax in a more social situation. You could try the following positive alternatives to smoking with the receptionist:

- Take a stroll outside your office building with a sip bottle of cool water;

- Take a cup of tea or coffee outside with you when you join the receptionist, instead of smoking with her;

- Mediate at your desk when you feel the tension overwhelm you;

- Sacrifice your friendship with the receptionist. If you cannot be with the receptionist while she smokes without having the urge to have a cigarette too, then the receptionist is your trigger. You must decide whether you want to spend time with her at the risk of continuing with your bad habit. Maybe you need to spend this time with a non-smoker work colleague.

You will know when you have found your new routine, because your mood will have altered from the norm whenever the urge takes a hold. By making a note of your mood after following the replacement routine, you can determine whether or not it is working for you. If it does not stop you from wanting to engage in the bad habit, it is probably not the answer to your problem. Try another routine. When you have found your new routine, use it as a substitute every time you come up against the bad habit trigger. With time and effort and endurance, you will be following the new routine automatically without consciously thinking about it.

Step 4: Replace every Trigger with a Positive Habit

This is really just a normal progression from step 2.

Strategy # 12: Prepare Your Plan to Break Your Bad Habit

Experiment during this time until you find your ideal placement habit. You will recognize it, because it will work for you, and you now need to work at aligning your behaviour according to the new activity rather than with the bad habit. You should do this systematically by having an alternative plan for every one of the triggers that you identified in the previous steps. You are reprogramming your brain to react to your urge with a new behaviour.

Using our receptionist illustration, you will reach for your chilled bottle of water or your hot drink when the receptionist signals for you to join her while she has her cigarette. Ideally you could get her to be your Accountability Partner, and together you can kick the smoking habit! If not, and you have decided that you can still be friends even if she continues to smoke while you are on your 30-day mission, you can enjoy your drink outside with her.

Easily said, but you might need some other ideas and strategies to get you through this stage of the habit changing. We have a few options, but we will concentrate on visualization over these 3 days:

Visualization is really just the adult word for what we knew as children to be daydreaming. Through visualizing you can successfully change your habit in your head, and you can overcome the onslaught of triggers very effectively. You will by now on your journey have bumped up against plenty of triggers, and you may have been sorely tempted to give in to them and accept the reward that follows. By picturing your new habit after each trigger, you can resist the urges through visualizing what you will achieve when you're successful.

You still don't know to, though. Let's use an example of scrolling through your social media whenever you feel bored, which is causing you way too much down time that you should be using towards more self-fulfilling acts. Through visualization, you replace the mobile phone in your hand when you're vegetating on the couch, with your laptop, writing that book you have always wanted to get written and published. You will need to recognize that boredom triggers your social media habit and catch it before you engage in the habit. Choose any new habit to implement whenever you feel bored if writing is not your passion. You could phone a friend, read a book or start a sketch.

You could also or rather visualize yourself dispelling the emotions that cause you to engage in your bad habit. Since your habit really rewards you in some way, ask yourself how you feel when you engage in the bad habit. Frustrated? Lonely? Bored? Cross? Imagine using your own thoughts as a means of reward to feel better instead of engaging in any kind of action. Let us use as an example feeling unable to cope with your workload. You resort to taking time out on social media whenever you face the impossibility of getting through your work by deadline instead of getting on with the work. Try visualizing yourself confronted by the work to be done, and gauge how you feel. Anxious? Stressed? Demotivated? Annoyed? How would you rather be feeling? Now imagine the feeling of being overburdened melting away, and your annoyance disappearing to be replaced by peace and a sense of calm. Imagine the new feeling slowly taking hold inside you. How do you feel now? Relaxed? Inspired? Confident? Artistic? Resolute? Let the new positive emotion take hold fully and allow yourself the time to let this happen without any pressure.

You can also use this technique of visualization to reinforce any new habits you would like to create. You simply have to repeat them in your mind, as many times as is necessary. Try imagining the routines or habits you would love to have. Now choose just one and focus on it during your process of visualization. Engage all your senses in creating an image of yourself taking action to ensure that it is as real as you can make it Now concentrate on whatever you see. Who is with you? How do you feel? Whatever you hear. Whatever you smell. Whatever it is that you are wearing.

The key to visualization is repetition. To establish a habit into your daily life, you should visualize regularly and as often as possible, until you have a clear image in your mind. Try out all the ways of visualizing until you find the one that works best for you, and then practice it until you have ditched whatever bad habits you focused on and replaced them with positive habits.

We will work more extensively on replacing every trigger with a positive habit during the third week of the 30-day plan.

Strategy # 13: Stay on Track Using Habit Reminders

Keep your habit change in mind all the time by somehow seeing to it that you are regularly prompted as to the habit you are breaking and the new habit you are instituting. Set alerts on your mobile phone or stick post its in your office or on your laptop as habit reminders to remind you to keep with your replacement or new routine.

Step 5: Create Rewards that Reward you in Return

Reward your routine in a way that inspires you to keep with the routine. For example, if you are aiming to break the habit of being too sedentary by getting fit, it will not do to reward yourself for completing s 20-minute run with 20 minutes on the computer. A more appropriate reward would be to buy yourself that pair of running shoes when you hit a certain target.

Strategy # 14: Reward Yourself

You need incentives to change, because we all know that change is hard. Rewards also serve to make the task of breaking your bad habit somehow fun. Set rewards for breaking your habit or changing your habit, and whenever you reach a specified milestone, make sure to reward yourself accordingly. You would do best by creating as many goals as is feasible and proactive. The more incentives you have, the more likely you will stay focused on breaking the habit. Set a goal for the first day, also set a goal for the first week and the second week. Of course you will need to reward yourself at the end of the 30 days. But you will also do well to have goals for the first and the third and the sixth months. And then a substantial reward for reaching your first-year anniversary! The more, the merrier. But they must be appropriate and reasonable goals and not simply rewards for the sake of rewarding.

On the subject of rewards, now would be a good time to give some advice on what not to reward yourself with. While your incentive should be relative to your goal, it should never be directly related to whatever activity you are actively removing from your life. In other words, do not reward weight loss with an all you can eat buffet. Rather reward weight loss with a new item of clothing in your new dress size. A good reward for reaching a fitness goal would be to treat yourself to a pair of those cute new yoga pants or training shoes.

Task 3:

1. Identify your triggers and write them down.

2. Identify your replacement habits and write them down.

3. Focus on applying the replacement habits every time you encounter your triggers.

4. Practice your visualization

5. Schedule at the start of each week, setting calendar alerts to get a cue that reminds you to engage in your target activity.

6. Set targets. Write them down and keep track of meeting them.

7. Write down the rewards for meeting each target.

Day Nine:
Set the Scene

Now that you have mastered the awareness stage and you are aware of the common patterns for your behaviour, you can go ahead and make the commitment to changing three, four or five aspects of your environment that will make it more difficult for you to engage in your bad habit. Make it hard to engage in the behaviour that you want to put a stop to. Getting rid of these external triggers and building your own barriers against your behaviour are way easier than having to constantly resist the temptation. Would you not rather do the hard work of making these small changes now so that you reduce the number of times you perform the habit, saving the scarce resource that is your willpower for those occasions where your control may be reduced.

Creating an environment which will make it easier for you to succeed is vital to you coming out of this 30-day plan triumphant and able to stick with the new habit for the duration and making the success long term. The more you can do to make sure that you are not doing this on willpower alone, the better. You do not and indeed cannot break habits or replace them with new habits reliant solely on willpower. It is way too hard. And it is also unnecessary. You are never going to trust an airline that flies in conditions that are not conducive to flying, are you? You should in fact be hard pressed to find such a commercial airline in the first place, Heaven help us. Why then would you want to live your life flying in the face of needless adversity?

To help you to form a habit, do all that you are able to make sure that the conditions in your environment are optimal. If you are chucking the habit of smoking and replacing it with exercising, for example, you would not be wanting to hang out with buddies who spend every free moment at the local pub, if your trigger is drinking. Hard as it may be, depending on your habit and where you are at with breaking it, you may even have to cut free certain of your friends. I'll give you a good example of this. Drug addicts often get hooked by a friend. You might be going through a tough time and a friend offers you something to take the edge off. Or you may have been in a bike accident which left you with injuries and debilitating and enduring pain, which addictive drugs helping with relief. If your friend is an enabler, sourcing and supplying you with the drugs that you have decided you do not want in your life anymore, then you need to not be around that friend in order to break that habit. Do you understand? Depending on the habit, you may have to implement some tough love with yourself to get through this. Often just the physical environment must change. It is only in very rare cases that a true friend will not support you in breaking your habit. Think about it....

Strategy # 15: Keep Away from Any and All Trigger Locations

It will help you a great deal to remain on track with changing your bad habit if you stay away from any places that might cause a negative habit loop while you are getting used to your 30-day plan. You will already have ascertained the locations that trigger your urge by now, which will make it easier for you to avoid them. If you are wanting to give up chocolate and you just know that those nights in front of the television watching a movie bring on the urge to snack on the sweet stuff. Try not to have chocolate in the house if you know you will be watching TV movies. And warn your friends not to bring any into the house either.

Task 4:

1. Write down at least 3 changes you need to make to your environment.

2. Modify your environment by writing down how you can decrease the steps between you and your replacement habit.

3. Write down how you can increase the steps between you and your bad habit.

4. Be hard on your friends. If they are not for you then they are against you. Write down the names of any friends or family

members you identify as those who will make it hard for you to break your habit.

5. Write down how you can put effective distance between yourself and the friends/family who won't support you kicking your bad habit.

6. Implement prompts to remind you to break the pattern through positive triggers that will keep you on track. E.g. putting your morning alarm across the room so that you have to get out of bed to turn it off will stop you hitting the snooze button.

Day Ten:
Support System

You cannot do this alone. Remember that you have to be tough on your friends and family, and even your co-workers. Anyone who might influence you while you are trying to break a habit and successfully replace the bad habit with a healthy habit. Tell everyone who has an interest in you and in you replacing your chosen bad habit with a healthy one about your chosen plan. The more supportive people you have in your corner during these 30 days and beyond, the better your chances for coming out the other side successful and keeping with the programme going forward.

Do not rely on your own volition during the period you are trying to break a bad habit. You do not need that kind of pressure. It is inevitable that you are going to want to relapse at some time, and this is when you need your support system and your friends to back you and keep you on the straight and narrow.

Recruit. If you do not have the friends you need to get you through this, go out and find a friend or a group that will work through it alongside you. If your new routine involves frequenting the gym, know that having a friend relying on you to join her for that class will make you get up and go to the gym on those days you really don't have the internal incentive to do so.

Task 5:

1. Tell everyone who has an interest in you about your plan to replace your chosen bad habit with a healthy one.

2. Join support groups if you need them to get your through.

Day Eleven:
Self-Talk

Get yourself a mantra. What is a mantra? The dictionary defines it as: 1. (originally in Hinduism and Buddhism) a word or sound repeated to aid concentration in meditation. (for example: "a mantra is given to a trainee meditator when his teacher initiates him." 2. a statement or slogan repeated frequently. (for example: "the environmental mantra that energy has for too long been too cheap." For the purpose of this exercise, however, the mantra would be a positive phrase, or an affirmative statement spoken out loud or repeated in your own mind to encourage or motivate yourself whenever needed. It must have the purpose of inspiring you to stick with your plan!

"Not One Puff Ever" is a good mantra to quit smoking. "Be a Man, Put Down the Can" works if you're a red-blooded man wanting to stop drinking.

Start to include the word "but" whenever negative self–talk threatens to overwhelm you. Negative self-talk is harmful, but it is remarkably easy to fall into the trap of judging yourself when you fall short of your goals. Whenever you are tempted to talk down to yourself or convince yourself that you suck when you make a mistake, add to your dialogue the word "but": I failed BUT we all fail sometimes. I am so fat BUT I have the chance to get into shape.

Task 6:

1. Get yourself a mantra and write it in your journal.

2. Practice your mantra whenever you feel that urge coming on to hit your bad habit.

3. Get into the habit of putting a but at the end of your negative self-talk.

Days Twelve, Thirteen, Fourteen, Fifteen and Sixteen: Meditation or Mindful Pauses

No, you really don't have to follow a guru or be into yoga to meditate for your own personal gain and wellbeing. If you, like many I know, have a mental block against the concept of meditation, it is just a word. Don't use the word if it pains you or does not sit well with your psyche. Think of it as Mindful Pauses. Meditation, or mindful pauses, are the foundation work for that long-term investment in yourself. Now that we have that out of the way, open your mind to the concept of meditating, or using mindful pauses, as a means of breaking a bad habit. Meditation or using mindful pauses is an excellent substitute for a bad habit. A replacement habit, if you will. Consistency is key with the practice of daily meditation (mindful pauses), and the basis for your progress. Start with just 5 minutes of meditation or building up your inner mindful pauses, with the aim of upping to 15 minutes, or as much as 30 minutes, if you think that is reasonable for you. Do not put pressure in yourself to increase your meditation time so that it becomes another thing you have to get done in your day rather than something you want to do. Five Minutes is good to get you going, and then go with your own flow to increase the time so that it suits you and your lifestyle and your needs. It will take you a lot longer than three days to master meditation or incorporating the art of incorporating mindful pauses, but the plan allows for you to concentrate on practicing meditation over these six days, without having to worry about mastering what is to follow just yet.

Bad habits very often start off as a means to counter boredom or to handle stress. If you can teach yourself to replace that bad habit with meditation, you will find breaking the habit so much simpler. When we talk of meditation, we are not suggesting you adopt the lotus position and remain so for an hour at a time. No. Not at all. Who has the time, and even fewer will be able to tuck their ankles in under their legs like you see the yogis and yoga enthusiasts managing to do? No. What we mean is practicing meditation over time to helps develop the ability to notice at the flick of a trigger the moment your mind becomes distracted. It gives you the time you need between your emotional trigger and your reaction, freeing you from your conditioned response. This in turn enables you to react better and way more effectively in the moment.

By way of example, let's take that moment when faced with the trigger of a drink in your hand and your response of automatically putting in a cigarette between your lips. Meditation, once you have the hang of it, allows you the calm perspective before lighting the cigarette in which to breathe, physically relax, and return the unlit cigarette to its pack. By taking control when you are in reactive mode, you can change your life by giving you the power in that moment from reacting to the trigger for the promise of the reward that is bad for you.

You will now interject every trigger you feel to lapse into your bad habit with a mindful pause. You do this simply by consciously using your art of self-talk to tell yourself whenever you feel the urge to engage in the bad habit: "I can engage in my bad habit, but first let me take a moment and just breathe deeply for 2 minutes."

Then for two minutes you can use your mantra or just breathe in and out slowly and deeply. Your breathing pattern should be long and even. When you breathe in, make sure that you fill your lungs properly. When you breathe out, allow all the air in your lungs to be expelled. Pay full and conscious attention, or rather be mindful to the sensation while you breathe. Feel the air as it moved through your body.

Re-evaluate after the two minutes and engage in the art of self-talk by asking: "How am I feeling right now?"

If the answer to this question is that you feel as if you no longer have the urge to engage in the bad habit, well done! You may feel that it is now somewhat more you feel you don't have the same urge anymore, or that it became more controllable and you do not have to engage in it. If this is the case, you should reward yourself because you have stopped your bad habit using mindfulness.

If the answer to the questions was that you still have the urge to engage in the habit, do so in a mindful way. Do not simply engage in the habit automatically, is what I am advocating. It is normal for the emotional trigger to wear off while you take two minutes to be mindful of it. You may need more time for this to take hold and that is okay. Just do not give up. Be mindful and you will succeed!

By pursuing the art of mindful pauses and meditation over these six days, you will have learned how they can help in your plan to break and change your habit in so many ways. Above all, you will have learnt to be more mindful, and you will notice your much-improved mental clarity. You will now have a useful tool to cope with stress. You will have exercised and strengthened your all-important willpower. You will have found healthy ways to fill those emotional gaps, and you will have had the opportunity and the resources to successfully re-condition your mind.

Meditation eases the battle of breaking habits with time and persistence, using willpower and the desire to succeed. Exercising your willpower much like you would a muscle, every day until you get it right, and believing in your commitment will make breaking that habit so much easier.

Task 7

1. Get the hang of meditating or interjecting mindful pauses into your day when you need them. On the first day of this stage, try to manage just 5 minutes.

2. As the days progress, up your meditating to 15 minutes and then work towards 30 minutes.

Days Seventeen-through-Twenty-Three: Behaviour Replacement

You need not view replacing the trigger as a fight. You can use it to your advantage by assigning a positive replacement behaviour to every trigger. We touched on visualization during the first week, and now you are ready to enhance this to your best advantage.

Visualize your trigger and feel the temptation pulling at your physically. Now replace that using whatever willpower is necessary to decide to choose your replacement habit over your bad habit. Do not stop visualizing until the urge has passed.

Only you can decide which behaviour replacement is best for you, though. I can give you some ideas and options, but you will need to figure out an alternative that works for your particular triggers and within your environments.

- If you have the urge to eat sweets after your evening meal, replace the sugary treats with one of your required servings of fruit or a chilled smoothie.

- If you simply cannot get going in the morning without your cup of coffee, try a hot cup of tea, and see if that helps. There are so many options.

- By the same token, if you are now an insomniac because you simply must have that cup of coffee close to your bedtime, replace it with a cup of chamomile tea. Add lemon and honey if that makes it more delightful. Or try a serving of hot milk with caffeine-free hot chocolate or Ovaltine.

- If you bite down on your jaw or grind your teeth in anxious situations, focus on your body and breathe in and out slowly until you feel more relaxed and able to control the stress.

- Are you an emotional shopper? Rather engage with friends or have a good TV program ready for when that trigger hits.

- If public speaking or even dealing one on one with a stranger causes you anxiety and urges you to smoke a cigarette or bite your nails or punctuate your speech with those annoying "uhms" or "you know," focus on pausing instead.

- When you are bored, ditch the addictive gaming online or scrolling through social media, and read a book instead. Or go to the gym, or exercise at home.

- If time management has become a problem because you habitually hit the snooze button every morning, try placing the alarm a few steps from the bed so that you have to get up. And then stay up and get on with your day.

If you can incorporate these behaviours, you are not only doing away with your bad habit, you are also developing good habits, which is absolutely optimal.

Task 8

1. Develop good habits while breaking your bad habit by practicing assigning a positive replacement behaviour to every trigger.

Days Twenty-four through Twenty-Nine: No Mercy

If you got this far then you are almost home free. During this last week you get to hone what you have learnt during the first three weeks. During this final stage you will master replacing the bad habit with the replacement habit all of the time. No exceptions. Practice your meditation, building it up to as long as you find personally optimal. These mindful pauses, once perfected, will stand you in good stead, and make is easier for you to adapt your environment. Adapting your environment and making the necessary changes also continues during this week, as you recognize more needs for change.

This is the week you determine whether you respond better to **positive or negative reinforcement** as a means to break your bad habit. You can try out such incentives as **aversion therapy**, or 'Push-Pull Motivation,' if you feel you need the added negative incentive to succeed. Let's delve more in depth into this form of conditioning of the brain.

Aversion therapy is helpful for those habit-changer wannabes who just cannot seem to do it without the help of some form of encouragement to change their routines. As with all things, different people have different ways of doing things and getting things done. Some people respond better to positive reinforcement while others are motivated by negative reinforcement. What does this mean?

Negative reinforcement is the bad consequence or aversive stimulus that does not happen when you engage in good behaviour. Quite simply, positive reinforcement involves a reward for succeeding or doing well. Think of positive reinforcement as that 'happy face' stamp in your workbook at school when you got through the exercise without mistakes as a youngster. On the other extreme, negative reinforcement is a penalty for not succeeding or for not getting it done as planned. But do not mistake this penalty as punishment. Negative reinforcement is certainly not the same as any form of punishment. As opposed to punishment, negative reinforcement is **not** being penalized for behaviour you were not meant to engage in. Negative reinforcement is being penalized for engaging in the bad behaviour. An example of punishment would be being spanked as a kid for misbehaving. Receiving a spot fine for parking in the wrong place is an example of negative reinforcement. You will not be parking there again if you can at all help it.

A popular tool while trying to break a habit employing the technique of aversion therapy or negative reinforcement is to wear a fairly staunch rubber band around the wrist. This is very much Pavlovian conditioning. To be able to break your habit, you must see to it that you do not like engaging in the habit anymore. You do this using aversive conditioning, which simply implements a process of inducing a negative stimulus in response to engaging in the bad habit. By experiencing the negative sensation at the same time as you do the bad habit, your brain will associate the one stimulus with the other, which will lead to you no longer enjoying or liking your bad habit. Whenever you find yourself relapsing into engaging in the bad habit, simply snap the rubber band (negative stimulus) fairly enthusiastically, so that a sharp pain is administered to the vulnerable soft underside of the wrist. The pro-negative reinforcers or aversion therapists now have the option of going techno with this rubber band concept, in the form of a self-shocking bracelet which administers a fairly serious shock. This is worn also around the wrist (bracelet style) and can be activated to self-shock the wearer whenever relapsing or engaging in the bad habit.

The bottom line of this type of reinforcement is association. Bad habit = Pain = Threat. Our little human brains, adaptable and impressive as they may be, do not operate very well with pain and threats. Certainly not the healthy specimens, anyway. The association of the bad habit with the promise or threat of pain is therefore a strong influencer and proponent of breaking bad habits. It is however not feasible to rely on long term, negative reinforcement to get the job done, which is why positive reinforcement must be brought back into the equation. Negative reinforcement works famously to get you started, whereas positive reinforcement or rewards see to it that you remain on track.

Let's give it a try, shall we:

- Step 1: You should be wearing your rubber band or the self-shocking bracelet. Now all you need to do is imagine that you are engaging in the bad habit, and then snap the band or activate the shock at the very same time.

- Step 2: Put the TRR process into play now. You should be referring back to the notes you made throughout the 30 day plan every day during the 30-day plan and beyond that, for as long as you need to. Select an alternative behaviour for your bad habit and implement that at least once a day during this phase. Be fully mindful of your craving. Now address that trigger using a reward other than your bad habit.

- Step 3: Ride the wave of your bad habit for a minimum of three minutes. Implement your alternative behaviour and of you still have the urge to do the bad habit after 10 minutes, then go ahead and do it. But you will feel so much better within yourself if you carry on resisting that urge for as long as it takes.

Discipline with Accountability may be just what you need to break that bad habit. You will benefit from this strategy if you are finding it impossible to get that new habit to stick. All it takes is to make the result of avoiding the new habit more uncomfortable than the satisfaction you experience from the reward you would get from engaging in the bad habit. Think of a brutal consequence you could try that would work for you. I could nudge you in the general direction with some illustrations:

- Every time you indulge in a sweet treat, you will spend 10 minutes on high intensity training;

- Every time you light up a cigarette, you will hand your wife your credit card for a lunch hour of shopping at will.

- Every time you skip a gym session, you will donate an hour's pay to a charity or cause that you absolutely disagree with.

Do not miss two in a row. The world will not fall off its axis if you miss one day, but if you miss the next day too, chances are really good that day 30 will spring itself on you and you will be devastated to realise that you failed dismally.

Task 9: This is a summary of all you had done so far

2. Master replacing your bad habit with the replacement habit all of the time, without exceptions.

3. Practice your meditation and/or mindful pauses so that you perfect it.

4. Adapt your environment and making whatever changes have shown themselves to be necessary.

5. Once you know whether negative reinforcement such as aversion therapy or 'Push-Pull Motivation, works for you or whether it is positive reinforcement that is going to get you through, work on it to make it work for you.

6. If you decide that Discipline with Accountability helps you to change your habit, improve on this strategy.

Day Thirty:
Strategize

Don't see this as the last day of your plan but the first day of doing this for the rest of your life. If you want to ditch the bad habit and keep the replacement habit, that is. You will need to beat the urge every single day forever. Life is never going to be without urges and you will just have to get the better of every one of them if you are going to be successfully bad habit free. And believe it, babe, urges are inevitable, and they are strong. But you are stronger, and every urge is temporary. Every urge is also so absolutely vanquishable. And so much fun to vanquish when you have followed your plan and you are in charge, strong and in control! The way to beat the urge is to remember that urges come in waves. Some stronger than others. Think of urges as waves on the beach. Think of yourself standing on the beach and watching the waves roll on to shore. Some waves will reach you. Some will chase you back or overwhelm you. Some will only wet your feet, maybe your ankles, maybe even your mid-calf. But the wave takes a while to roll in and is only on the beach for a moment before it ebbs. The urge will only last one or two minutes at most. All that is required for you to do to vanquish the wave is to ride it out. Just ride the wave, and the urge will ebb and that will be the end of that particular wave or urge.

As always, it may be easier said than done. That is where the strategies make themselves known. You will need to strategize if you are going to always make it through every urge.

How? Try these strategies:

- mindful pauses or meditation,

- deep breathing,

- exercise – it doesn't have to be hectic. Try skipping rope just for a few seconds,

- go for a stroll,

- pop frozen grapes or chilled strawberries into your mouth and savour,

- self-massage,

- sip on a bottle or glass of fresh water,

- call in your support – ring a friend or connect with your support network in whichever way you prefer.

In order to beat the challenges that you will undoubtably encounter while trying to break your bad habits, you might want to try these strategies to overcome what is known as the hot-cold empathy gap and come out the other side of any moment of weakness or temptation successfully:

Strategy #16: Know About the Hot-Cold Empathy Gap

While plans are great on paper, they do have their fault lines in real life. Just like most paradise spots on earth have a fault line that causes them to be prey to natural disasters over which they have no control. but they always emergency strategies in place. It is very difficult to stay true to any new routine when you are tired, hungry, depressed or under unrelenting pressure of any kind. Not to mention those pesky omnipresent triggers.

So what does George Loewenstein's discovery known as the Hot-Cold Empathy Gap have to do with you and breaking bad habits? George discovered in his tireless studies that humans are quite incapable of using planning as a means to better understand how we will feel when faced with any form of intense craving. What this means for you in your 30-day plan and beyond is that you will just have to strategize for dealing with slip-ups. And slip-ups are just mistakes, and mistakes will happen. To err is, after all, human. Slip-ups do not mean you are weak and succumbing to desires every once in a while, is just part of permanently changing a habit.

Strategy # 17: Stay Positive

As pointed out in strategy # 16, temptations are all perfectly natural in the great scheme of things while you are in the process of breaking bad habits and implementing healthy habits in their stead. So chin up! You can get through this by using your commitment. Every time you are faced with a trigger or a cue that would lead to your engaging in the bad habit, recommit to staying true to the plan to break that habit.

Remember to use your mantra if you feel about to cave in. Repeat it as often as you need to get your through the hard times.

Strategy # 18: The "What-the-Hell Effect" is your boogie man

Failure is par for the course when you are breaking a bad habit. Your big enemy here is the what the hell mindset sneaking up and ambushing you. With this mindset you simply throw in the towel and go on a binge because, what the hell, you have already failed. Just remember that the sun will come up tomorrow, and you get to try again. Accept your failure and get to the business of damage control and reducing any resultant fall out. Never ever resort to using this as an excuse to slip up again, though.

Strategy # 19: Self-Forgiveness

Falling off the wagon is a great forerunner to throwing in the towel when trying to change a habit because people just do not know how to get back on the horse (or the wagon) again. Instead of giving up on the plan when it goes awry, often many weeks into a largely successful exercise, why not just try to forgive yourself. It's been said before and I will say it again: to err is human, to forgive, divine. Be divine. No good will come of getting all tough with yourself over a slip-up. Negative thoughts are not helpful when trying to bring about a lasting change.

Strategy # 20: Adopt a Healthy Lifestyle

With ego depletion a constant threat to your willpower, temptation is a very real risk when you are weakened: hungry, tired, depressed or stressed. Your best weapon against ego depletion is to adopt a healthy lifestyle, using steps such as:

Be well rested. Get between 6- and 9-hours' good sleep every night so that you are properly energized for your day.

Hydrate! Eight glasses of water daily seems to be the agreed upon magic number but you should be the best one to determine your personal needs. Be realistic.

Make sure to eat a balanced meal every day, incorporating enough servings of fresh fruit and vegetables, lean protein and the good kind of carbohydrates. Also have healthy snacks in reach at all times so that you can beat that hunger without the sweet treats. You may also just be thirsty when you think you are hungry so try sipping your water first. That might help.

Strategy # 21: Naysayers are Non-Players

Watch out for poison dwarves. No, these are not figments of myth. They really do exist, and you will find at least one while you are executing your 30-day plan. The name is derived from the German 'Giftzwerg' which is made up of the German word for poison, which is "gift-" and "-Zwerg". Zwerg is in fact a creature of myth, which we have duly anglicized to "dwarf". Giftzwerg very aptly describes an unpleasant or obnoxious person. These omnipresent poison dwarves are small in mind but always around. You will always have at least one person (if you are very fortunate, only one) who will either subconsciously or consciously do whatever is in their misguided power to sink your attempts at making that vital change for your own betterment. You will only have to lend them an ear to put yourself at real risk of failure. Poisoned dwarves need not be just close friends or family members. Complete strangers are also more than willing and able to sink your ship, drowning out all your good efforts with remarks that breed self-limiting thoughts. Handling naysayers is as important as having a plan to overcome an urge. Always have a suitable come-back to whatever they have to throw at you. Make it a game. You can even write some ideas down as they come to you and then make a plan to remember them so that you have the ammunition when the enemy attacks.

You will need to be ever vigilant of **saboteurs**, in whatever form they appear. They will always be there and there will usually be at least one. Negative people are a big obstacle to breaking habits and replacing them with new ones. In fact, negative people are a major and significant hindrance to any self-improvement attempt, whatever it may be. Saboteurs are really adept at getting you to fall back on your bad habits. We can't explain why. It is just one of those life manifestations that you simply have to cope with the best way you can. What you need to be prepared to do in your strategy against being sabotaged is to be ready. Confront the saboteur directly. Let them know that you would be pleased to have their support. If they are quite sure that they cannot be supportive of your attempts, then you would very much appreciate it if they got out of your way. Make it part of your plan not to have them around, if that is what it is going to take.

Strategy # 22: Manage One Day at A Time

Keep your eye on the ball and you may not be as easily bowled over. Watch out for that potential trigger or cue and focus on your plan for today only. Tomorrow is always only a day away, and there is nothing you can do now about what might or might not come along in the future. This is the best way to get those small changes under your belt without looking at the bigger picture before the time is right. That permanent change to your routine will one day become evident, and you will probably be surprised because you did not even see it coming. Before you known it, instead of looking out for the triggers, you are already resisting the urges.

Strategy # 23: Analyse Your Plan Every Day

Remember that commitment we mentioned at the start of the book? Well, here it is again. Commitment and reminders absolutely have to be checked every day if you are going to have any hope at all of sticking with your 30-day plan. Bear in mind that what you are doing by attempting to break your bad habit is just the same as attempting any long-term goal. Provided you see your habit change as a goal that must be reviewed every day, you should successfully master the 30-day plan. Your daily commitment requires you to remain focused and not to stress the small stuff. Slip ups are part of the journey, so just keep going, learn from every trigger and urge that comes along, and soon enough you will have replaced that bad habit with a healthy habit.

Strategy # 24: Get Professional Support

Real problems need real solutions. In the case of a serious addiction that is harmful and possibly a threat to your wellbeing and that of your significant others, a higher level of expertise far beyond a 30-day self-designed plan may be just what the doctor ordered, so to say. Unfortunately there is no definite line drawn as far as what you can and cannot deal with personally without professional support, so you will just have to know that you have the knowledge and the integrity to figure this out for yourself. Listen to your significant others if they suggest you need outside help, though. Generally speaking, drug addiction, alcoholism, chain-smoking, eating disorders and binge eating might be among those you could look into getting professional support to overcome, beat and replace. In some instances support groups that form part of regular meetings or a group therapy arrangement might be what is called for. You might consider:

- Discussing your issue with a counsellor, therapist, psychologist or psychiatrist

- Find groups in your area that focus on support for your specific habit, such as Alcoholics Anonymous or Narcotics Anonymous

- Try that local weekly Weighless or Weightwatchers meeting or any similar group that focuses on permanent lifestyle changes

- See your general practitioner for advice on how to overcome unhealthy cravings

Task 10:

1. Remember that urges are temporary and work at pushing through each one as it hits, using the strategies you have selected.

2. Use your chosen strategies to overcome the hot-cold empathy gap.

3. User your commitment to stay positive.

4. Practice your mantra and use it when you need to.

5. Avoid the What-the-Hell mindset.

6. Take time to take care of yourself: practice self-forgiveness, get enough rest, eat properly and stay hydrated.

7. Exercise your strategy to work around Nay-Sayers and saboteurs if you cannot avoid them entirely.

8. Take every day as it comes and don't stress about tomorrow.

9. Seek out professional help or support if you find that you simply cannot beat this on our own.

Once you understand that changing a behaviour cannot be achieved in a day or even in two days, you will recognize the need for a plan. Long term changes need long term plans, and you now have the ammunition and the knowledge to go out there and achieve. You can do it....

February 2015

Mon, Feb 16 - Sun, Feb 22

Wk 1 to Wk 4

	February 2015					
Su	Mo	Tu	We	Th	Fr	Sa
1	2	3	4	5	6	7
8	9	10	11	12	13	14
15	16	17	18	19	20	21
22	23	24	25	26	27	28

	March 2015					
Su	Mo	Tu	We	Th	Fr	Sa
1	2	3	4	5	6	7
8	9	10	11	12	13	14
15	16	17	18	19	20	21
22	23	24	25	26	27	28
29	30	31				

Important Dates

✓	ABC	Prioritized Task List

$Amt	Budget Cat.	$Bal.

✓	Qty	To Buy

Monday, February 16, 2015
Presidents' Day

Carbs

Water

Exercise

Meals
B
L
D

7:00
8:00
9:00
10:00
11:00
12:00
1:00
2:00
3:00
4:00
5:00
6:00
7:00
8:00
9:00

Tuesday, February 17, 2015
Mardi Gras

Carbs

Water

Exercise

Meals
B
L
D

7:00
8:00
9:00
10:00
11:00
12:00
1:00
2:00
3:00
4:00
5:00
6:00
7:00
8:00
9:00

Wednesday, February 18, 2015
Ash Wednesday

Carbs

Water

Exercise

Meals
B
L
D

7:00
8:00
9:00
10:00
11:00
12:00
1:00
2:00
3:00
4:00
5:00
6:00
7:00
8:00
9:00

Reminders		People to Contact	

Thursday, February 19, 2015	Friday, February 20, 2015	Saturday, February 21, 2015	Sunday, February 22, 2015
Chinese New Year			

Calorie

Water

Exercise

Meals
B
L
D

	Thursday	Friday	Saturday	Sunday
7				
8				
9				
10				
11				
12				
1				
2				
3				
4				
5				
6				
7				
8				
9				

A helpful addition to your 30-day plan is a tangible template much like the one above. You can use an app on your mobile, or a desk calendar or wall planner. But you need to write down your plan.

When you have your plan written out, make sure to include the tasks for the 30 days.

TASKS

Task 1: Days 1 to 3

1. Have a journal designated to breaking the habit and write down everything during the 30 days.

2. Write down the habit you have selected to break.

3. Submit your detailed plan to paper because you will have to refer to the plan throughout the 30 days and for a long time beyond. Include:

   a. possible obstacles,

   b. triggers,

   c. support system

   d. support buddies, and

   e. how you plan to succeed

10. What is your primary motivation for breaking this bad habit? Write it down.

11. Write down the top ten negative side effects of your bad habit

12. Write down the top ten positive changes that would come with breaking this bad habit

13. Write down the top ten excuses you would typically fall back on to justify your bad habit

14. Develop your self-awareness about what your internal and the external triggers are. Take note of and be aware of where and when your bad habit is triggered:

    a. At what time/s of the day/night?

    b. Where are you?

    c. Who are you with? Are you with someone?

    d. What triggers the start of the behaviour?

    e. How do you feel immediately before the urge to engage in the habit?

    f. How do you feel physically both during and after giving in to the urge?

15. Make a separate list of the possible obstacles you mentioned in (3) above. Beside each, note what you will do to minimize or avoid them.

16. Read your list and your plan as often as you need to until you have an impression in your own mind explaining your reasons for having to break your bad habit.

Task 2: Day 4 and 5

1. Decide the optimal amount of sleep you need nightly to perform at your peak. Write it down in your designated journal. Tip – it should be no less than 7 hours and no more than 9 hours. Write down the amount of sleep you get every night

2. How much water do you usually drink? If it is less than 500ml, make a commitment to increase it to at least 1250ml before moving onto the next phase, and up to 2000ml within the week. Make a note of the amount of water you drink every day.

3. Write down the steps you will take to improve your posture and check against it every day.

Task 3: Days 6 to 8

1. Identify your triggers and write them down.

2. Identify your replacement habits and write them down.

3. Focus on applying the replacement habits every time you encounter your triggers.

4. Practice your visualization

5. Schedule at the start of each week, setting calendar alerts to get a cue that reminds you to engage in your target activity.

6. Set targets. Write them down and keep track of meeting them.

7. Write down the rewards for meeting each target.

Task 4: Day 9

1. Write down at least 3 changes you need to make to your environment.

2. Modify your environment by writing down how you can decrease the steps between you and your replacement habit.

3. Write down how you can increase the steps between you and your bad habit.

4. Be hard on your friends. If they are not for you then they are against you. Write down the names of any friends or family members you identify as those who will make it hard for you to break your habit.

5. Write down how you can put effective distance between yourself and the friends/family who won't support you kicking your bad habit.

6. Implement prompts to remind you to break the pattern through positive triggers that will keep you on track. E.g. putting your morning alarm across the room so that you have to get out of bed to turn it off will stop you hitting the snooze button.

Task 5: Day 10

1. Tell everyone who has an interest in you about your plan to replace your chosen bad habit with a healthy one.

2. Join support groups if you need them to get your through.

Task 6: Day 11

1. Get yourself a mantra and write it in your journal.

2. Practice your mantra whenever you feel that urge coming on to hit your bad habit.

3. Get into the habit of putting a but at the end of your negative self-talk.

Task 7: Days 12 to 16

1. Get the hang of meditating or interjecting mindful pauses into your day when you need them. On the first day of this stage, try to manage just 5 minutes.

2. As the days progress, up your meditating to 15 minutes and then work towards 30 minutes.

Task 8: Days 17 to 23

1. Develop good habits while breaking your bad habit by practicing assigning a positive replacement behaviour to every trigger.

Task 9: Days 24 to 29

2. Master replacing your bad habit with the replacement habit all of the time, without exceptions.

3. Practice your meditation and/or mindful pauses so that you perfect it.

4. Adapt your environment and making whatever changes have shown themselves to be necessary.

5. Once you know whether negative reinforcement such as aversion therapy or 'Push-Pull Motivation, works for you or whether it is positive reinforcement that is going to get you through, work on it to make it work for you.

6. If you decide that Discipline with Accountability helps you to change your habit, improve on this strategy.

Task 10: Day 30

1. Remember that urges are temporary and work at pushing through each one as it hits, using the strategies you have selected.

2. Use your chosen strategies to overcome the hot-cold empathy gap.

3. User your commitment to stay positive.

4. Practice your mantra and use it when you need to.

5. Avoid the What-the-Hell mindset.

6. Take time to take care of yourself: practice self-forgiveness, get enough rest, eat properly and stay hydrated.

7. Exercise your strategy to work around Nay-Sayers and saboteurs if you cannot avoid them entirely.

8. Take every day as it comes and don't stress about tomorrow.

9. Seek out professional help or support if you find that you simply cannot beat this on our own.

DISCLAIMER

The opinions and ideas of the author contained in this publication are designed to educate the reader in an informative and helpful manner. While we accept that the instructions will not suit every reader, it is only to be expected that the recipes might not gel with everyone. Use the book responsibly and at your own risk. This work with all its contents, does not guarantee correctness, completion, quality or correctness of the provided information. Always check with your medical practitioner should you be unsure whether to follow a low carb eating plan. Misinformation or misprints cannot be completely eliminated. Human error is real!

Picture: Baranov E // www.shutterstock.com

Design: Natalia Design

Printed in Poland
by Amazon Fulfillment
Poland Sp. z o.o., Wrocław